INVENTIONS THAT CHANGED THE WORLD

ALEXANDER GRAHAM BELL

and the TELEPHONE

Louise Spilsbury

PowerKiDS press

NEW YORK

J.T.B. DEL.

Published in 2016 by **The Rosen Publishing Group**
29 East 21st Street, New York, NY 10010

Produced for Rosen by Calcium

Editors for Calcium: Harriet McGregor and Sarah Eason
Designers: Jessica Moon and Paul Myerscough
Picture Research: Harriet McGregor

Picture credits: Cover: AP Images: AP Photo (fg); Getty Images: Universal History Archive (bkgd).
Insides: Dreamstime: Dvmsimages 11, Georgios Kollidas 5, 28; Library of Congress: Gilbert
H. Grosvenor Collection, Prints and Photographs Division 6, 20–21, Richard W. Sears 13, 29;
Shutterstock: Everett Historical 15, 16, 17, 19, 21, 23, 25, Morphart Creation 7, Ralf Siemieniec 24,
ValeStock 26–27b, Wrangler 26–27t; Wellcome Library, London: 10; Wikimedia Commons: 8, 9, 12.

Cataloging-in-Publication Data
Spilsbury, Louise.
Alexander Graham Bell and the telephone / by Louise Spilsbury.
p. cm. — (Inventions that changed the world)
Includes index.
ISBN 978-1-5081-4623-0 (pbk.)
ISBN 978-1-5081-4624-7 (6-pack)
ISBN 978-1-5081-4625-4 (library binding)
1. Bell, Alexander Graham, — 1847-1922 — Juvenile literature.
2. Inventors — United States — Biography — Juvenile literature.
3. Telephone — United States — History — Juvenile literature.
I. Spilsbury, Louise. II. Title.
TK6143.B4 S65 2016
621.385—d23

Manufactured in the United States of America
CPSIA Compliance Information: Batch #BW16PK: For Further Information contact Rosen Publishing, New York, New York at 1-800-237-9932

CONTENTS

THE POWER OF THE TELEPHONE

When Alexander Graham Bell invented the first practical, working telephone he assured himself a place in the history books forever. The telephone was an invention that truly changed the world. It quickly became the fastest and most efficient way for people to communicate over any distance.

BEFORE THE TELEPHONE

Communicating across long distances took a long time before the telephone was invented. Letters were carried by horses and riders or wagons, and it could take days to deliver them. Ships used flags to send signals and communicate with each other across stretches of the ocean. The invention of the **telegraph** allowed people to send messages using signals and code much more quickly, but only through a telegraph operator, so it was still impossible to speak privately and directly with another person. It was not until 1876, when Alexander Graham Bell developed a successful telephone, that a new world of communication opened up. People could speak and hear each other through wires that connected them in a completely new way.

KEEPING IN TOUCH

Today, almost everyone has a phone and most of us carry our phones with us at all times, so we are never out of touch with friends and family. We can use our phones to speak to someone nearby or on the other side of the world. People use their phones for work and to call for help in emergencies, such as when a car breaks down. Emergency calls can be made in the remotest places, so the telephone can even save lives. It is hard to imagine what life was like before the telephone was invented.

The Word Is...

Was Alexander's invention the result of a mistake? When he was a student, Alexander was intrigued by a German book about making vowel sounds using electrical tuning forks. Alexander's German was not great and he mistakenly translated this to say that vowel sounds could be transmitted "over a wire." Alexander later said:

"It gave me confidence. If I had been able to read German, I might never have begun my experiments in **electricity**."

EARLY YEARS

Alexander Graham Bell was born in Edinburgh, Scotland, on March 3, 1847. He was the second of three sons born to Alexander Melville Bell and Eliza Grace Symonds. His mother was deaf and his father was a professor of speech **elocution** at the University of Edinburgh.

HOMESCHOOLED

Until the age of 11, Alexander was taught at home and spent a lot of time with his family. His father's interest in elocution and his mother's hearing difficulties had a big effect on Alexander. He was fascinated by how sounds were made and heard. While his brothers spoke to their mother through an **ear trumpet** that increased the volume of their voices, Alexander discovered that by speaking with his mouth on his beloved mother's forehead she could hear him through the **vibrations** his sounds made. At 11, he entered the Royal High School at Edinburgh and studied there for four years. Although he was good at science, Alexander did not enjoy school and he left when he was 15.

This photograph shows five-year-old Alexander (second from right) with his father, mother, and brothers.

EARLY INVENTIONS

Alexander may not have been very successful at school, but he was already showing signs of genius. When he was just 12 years old, he visited

A Speaking Machine

On a trip to London, Alexander and his father visited Charles Wheatstone to see his speaking machine. When bellows pushed air through a leather tube and past a vibrating reed, Wheatstone could squeeze the tube and produce sounds like words. Back in Edinburgh, Alexander and his brother Melville made their own speaking machine. They made a head with movable jaws and a tongue with a tin tube for a throat. Two pieces of rubber acted as vocal cords. When the brothers blew through the tin tube, the rubber vibrated and made sound waves. By moving the "mouth," they shaped the sound waves into humanlike sounds.

a flour mill owned by a friend's father and noticed that taking the outer husks off the wheat grains took workers a long time. So, he invented a machine that removed the husks using paddles and nail brushes that rotated and brushed off the husks. The mill owner was impressed and gave Alexander and his friend a small space in his mill to use as a workshop.

In the mid nineteenth century, Edinburgh was a hotbed of scientific and technological ideas. This must have inspired Alexander to become an inventor who could change the world.

TEACHING SPEECH

At the age of 16, Alexander was teaching music and elocution at a boy's boarding school in Scotland. After his family moved to London in 1865, he took up his studies again at University College. Unfortunately, tragedy was about to strike his family and bring about another dramatic move.

Alexander's future wife, Mabel, was 16 when they met at a school for the deaf where he taught.

COMING TO AMERICA

In 1867, Alexander's younger brother Edward died of an illness called tuberculosis, and just three years later his older brother Melville suffered the same fate. Shortly afterward, the family, still in deep mourning, moved to Canada. Alexander's parents believed the climate there was better than in Scotland and would keep Alexander, their only remaining son, from getting sick too. They settled in Brantford, Ontario, but in April 1871, Alexander moved to Boston to teach at the Boston School for Deaf Mutes. He also taught at schools in Massachusetts and Connecticut.

FRIENDS AND FAMILY

Alexander's teaching work taught him a great deal about sounds and hearing, and also brought him into contact with some of the most important people in his future life. In the fall of 1872, Alexander opened his own private school for the deaf in Boston. One of his first pupils was George Sanders, the deaf son of Thomas and Sarah Sanders. Thomas Sanders became a great friend and later an important **investor** in Alexander's telephone company. In 1873, another pupil, a young woman named Mabel Hubbard, who had been deaf since catching scarlet fever at the age of five, joined the school. As they worked together, she and Alexander fell in love. They later married in 1877.

Alexander (top right) with some of his deaf pupils in Boston, Massachusetts.

Visible Speech

At first, Alexander used his father's method of helping deaf people speak, called visible speech. The system of visible speech consisted of a chart of symbols to help people say words, even if they had never heard them. Each symbol represented a sound made by the human voice. Different parts of each symbol showed deaf pupils how to pronounce different sounds. Alexander had toured Scotland with his brothers demonstrating this method, and his father toured the United States demonstrating it, too. Later, Alexander used his own methods of teaching speech and **lipreading** to deaf children.

EXPERIMENTS IN SOUND

A lexander was teaching and working as a university professor at Boston University during the daytime, but he could not resist continuing to create inventions at night.

HARMONIC TELEGRAPHS

In the 1870s, telegraph was the only way people could communicate over long distances. Messages were sent using a series of electrical clicks, known as **Morse Code**, along cables that had been laid around the world.

Antonio Meucci built a wired communication device so that his sick wife could call him.

Rival Inventors

Some people believe that Italian-American inventor Antonio Meucci invented a telephone device before Alexander. In 1856, he linked wires from his workshop to his sick wife's bedroom so she could call him if she needed help. However, Antonio could not afford to buy a **patent** for his voice communication machine. Inventors take out a patent on their new invention so that other people cannot copy it without permission. Antonio died before he could prove that his discovery had been made before Alexander's.

Laying cables was expensive so inventors were trying out new ways to send several messages at the same time along the same cable. Alexander started working on designs that could divide a telegraph line into 10 or more channels, called a harmonic telegraph. To carry on with his research, Alexander needed money to pay for his time and equipment. Luckily, his father-in-law, Gardiner Hubbard, an old friend Thomas Sanders, and lawyer Anthony Pollok were wealthy and willing to support him while he worked on the harmonic telegraph.

A BREAKTHROUGH

The money allowed Alexander to hire Thomas Watson, a skilled electrical engineer, to work with him and together they began work in earnest. It was when working on a harmonic telegraph that Alexander had his first breakthrough. While Alexander was trying to send several sounds over the telegraph, Thomas heard the sound of a reed being plucked from the other end of a line. They used this knowledge to build their first telephone, known as the Gallows phone. It could not transmit words as they had hoped it would, but it made Alexander ever more determined to succeed.

This device is a replica, or copy, of Alexander's first Gallows telephone, invented in 1875.

EUREKA!

The harmonic telegraphs Alexander worked on used reeds or tuning forks that responded to different high and low sounds. After a lifetime of working with sound and speech, Alexander knew that it was only a small step from sending musical notes through a harmonic telegraph to transmitting the human voice. So in 1875, when Alexander was 27, he decided to take out a patent for transmitting speech over an electrical wire.

Elisha Gray invented a telephone too, but Alexander registered his patent first.

The Word Is...

The first words ever spoken on the telephone were spoken by Alexander to his assistant, Thomas Watson:

"I then shouted into M [the mouthpiece] the following sentence: 'Mr. Watson, come here, I want to see you!' To my delight he came and declared that he had heard and understood what I said."

A RACE AGAINST TIME

Alexander applied for his first patent in the United Kingdom and, after it had been granted there, planned to apply in the United States, too. When he applied, he still had not invented a working telephone. In February 1876, rival inventor Elisha Gray applied for a US patent for a telephone that used salt water to transmit sound waves. Alexander filed his US patent application on the same day. In March 1876, Alexander and Thomas had their most important breakthrough: they transmitted the human voice through wires between different rooms in a house. Like Elisha's invention, Alexander's also used a liquid to transfer sound waves, so Elisha argued that he had stolen his idea. However, Alexander used a different liquid and had made a working telephone before Elisha, so it was Alexander who won the race to become the inventor of the telephone.

Alexander (right) in 1916, unveiling a plaque commemorating the invention of the telephone.

HOW IT WORKED

Throughout his years of work with sound and hearing, Alexander knew that human speech came in wavelike patterns. He believed that he could carry human speech through wires if he could produce an electrical wave that could follow the same patterns as the human voice.

HOW SOUND WAVES WORK

To understand how Alexander's first telephone worked, it helps to know a little about how sound waves work. A sound happens when something vibrates. Vibrations are movements backward and forward, or up and down. When something vibrates, whether it is a string on a guitar or a ruler twanged against a desk, it makes the air around it vibrate, too. It is these air vibrations that are called sound waves. People hear sounds when sound waves travel through the air and reach their ears. The ears turn them into signals that the brain can interpret as different sounds.

ALEXANDER'S LIQUID TELEPHONE

With his new telephone, Alexander had discovered a way to make electric **currents** mimic sound waves. A current is the flow of electricity through a wire. Alexander's first telephone used liquid **acid** as a transmitter. His telephone had a cone or funnel-shaped part that focused sounds onto a circle of paper. This circle of paper was stretched over a frame. A needle connected the paper with a small cup of acid. When Alexander spoke into the funnel, sound waves made the paper vibrate. The vibrating paper made the needle move in the acid. The tiny vibrations in the acid changed the current in an electric wire. At the other end of the wire an identical system reversed the process, to change the vibrations back into words.

Phone Faults

It is thought that Alexander's famous first words, "Mr. Watson, come here, I want to see you!" were a cry for help. When Alexander was connecting the parts of his phone, he accidentally spilled acid onto his pants. When Thomas came running to Alexander saying he had heard every word, Alexander forgot about the acid on his pants! He realized, though, that he would have to make a telephone without liquid if other people were to use it!

TELEPHONES TAKE OFF

Alexander was delighted to have made such a breakthrough and spent the next few months improving his telephone so it could work without acid or liquid, and be used by the public. One of his new, improved versions was known as the butterstamp telephone, because it looked like the device used to stamp patterns onto the pats of butter used at that time.

THE BUTTERSTAMP TELEPHONE

The butterstamp telephone used an **electromagnet** instead of liquid to change sound waves into electric currents. An electromagnet is a metal that becomes magnetic when electricity flows through it. The butterstamp telephone was made of wood and contained a magnet, a coil of wire, and a thin iron disk. When someone spoke into it, different sound waves made the disk vibrate in different ways.

By 1885, fewer than 10 years after Alexander invented the telephone, operators like this one were connecting calls for the American Telephone and Telegraph Company.

This continuously changed the electric signal that flowed through wires to the handset at the other end of the machine. The second handset turned the message back into sounds.

EXCHANGES AND OPERATORS

Once telephones were ready for people to use, some businesses and rich people ran wires between themselves and the people they wanted to talk to. These were called direct lines. However, most early telephones were used by businesses or connected to an important local building, such as a police station, doctor's office, or bank. Telephone exchanges were set up to connect different lines. To make a call, a person phoned the operator and they connected that person's wire to other wires, by hand through a switchboard. When the conversation was over, the operator would disconnect the wires again. If someone wanted a phone at home, he or she could pay a monthly fee to the switchboard to use the telephone network, too.

By 1914, soldiers fighting in World War I (1914–1918) were able to contact their commanders using a telephone.

Improving the Telephone

The butterstamp telephone only had a disk and electromagnet at one end, so people had to talk into the handset and then move it to their ear to hear a reply. By the 1890s, many telephones had two parts: one that contained a **transmitter** to speak into and one that contained the **receiver** through which people could listen.

FAME AND FORTUNE

At first, many people thought that Alexander's invention was a passing fad, and some even laughed at it! How wrong they were. The invention of the telephone changed the world forever and brought Alexander both fame and fortune.

FAMOUS FACES

In June 1876, Alexander demonstrated his telephone at the Philadelphia Centennial Exhibition, an important national show in the United States. Some of the judges seemed uninterested in Alexander's invention, but then it was tested by the Emperor of Brazil, Dom Pedro II. When the emperor heard it working, he cried out: "My God, it talks!" By August 1876, Alexander was on the receiving end of the first long-distance call, transmitted from Brantford to nearby Paris, Ontario. Alexander and his invention made the newspapers and his fame quickly spread. In 1878, Alexander was even invited to demonstrate his remarkable telephone to Queen Victoria of England.

MAKING MONEY

Toward the end of 1876, Alexander and his investors tried to sell the patent for the telephone to Western Union for $100,000. Western Union was the biggest communications company in North America and ran the country's telegraph system. The company refused because they thought the telephone would not make money! Western Union soon realized their mistake and tried to buy the patent in 1878, but it was too late. In July 1877, Gardiner Hubbard had organized a group to set up the Bell Telephone Company to sell Alexander's telephone. Alexander was given one-third of the company's shares and made its technical advisor. The telephone was a huge success and Alexander soon became very rich.

The Word Is...

Alexander was a great believer in hard work and determination. He said:

"A man, as a general rule, owes very little to what he is born with; a man is what he makes of himself."

By 1899, telephones were selling well and the ability to build a telephone was a very useful skill for any young person looking for work.

FAMILY AND RETIREMENT

On July 11, 1877, Alexander married his beloved Mabel Hubbard at last, and they set off on a honeymoon to England that lasted two years. While they were there, Alexander continued to demonstrate the telephone, but he was losing interest in his first major invention.

MOVING ON

In 1880, Alexander sold most of his shares and retired from the Bell Telephone Company. He had little involvement with the company from then on, concentrating instead on new inventions and his family. In 1879, Alexander and Mabel returned to Canada, bringing with them their first daughter, who was named Elsie. A second daughter, named Marian but known as Daisy, was born in 1880. Sadly, although the couple also had two sons, both boys died not long after they were born.

SETTING UP LABS

Alexander and his family moved to Washington, D.C., in 1880. In that same year, the French Government awarded Alexander the Volta Prize for the invention of the telephone.

Alexander with his wife Mabel and their children Elsie (left) and Marian in around 1885.

He used the prize money to set up Volta Associates and build a laboratory that would focus on the research of recording and transmitting sound. Then, in 1885, the Bells visited Cape Breton Island in Baddeck, Nova Scotia. They loved it so much that they built a home there, first for summer vacations and later to live in permanently. There at last was a place where Alexander could live in peace and devote all the time he wanted to his work. He had a laboratory and a study where he could work. When he was out walking he kept a personal notebook in the pocket of his favorite jacket, so he could write down new ideas whenever they came to him.

Alexander's iron lung invention helped polio patients breathe when the condition paralyzed muscles in their chest.

An Inspired Invention

One of Alexander's sons died because he had severe breathing problems. This inspired Alexander to invent a metal jacket that could help people with breathing problems breathe. An improved version of Alexander's metal jacket, or **respirator**, was known as the iron lung. This iron cylinder fitted around a patient's chest and a pump forced air in and out, making the patient's own lungs work.

MORE INVENTIONS

Inventing the telephone made Alexander rich and famous, but he needed new challenges to hold his interest. Over the next few decades, he came up with some truly amazing inventions.

PHOTOPHONES

In 1880, Alexander took out a patent on an invention called the photophone. This was the first wireless telephone because it was able to transmit sound on a beam of light instead of electrical wires. Alexander and his assistant Tainter managed to transmit a voice message over 650 feet (200 m) in Washington. They also made improvements to Thomas Edison's invention of the phonograph, which was designed to record and reproduce sound.

METAL DETECTOR

In July 1881, US President James Garfield was shot and doctors could not locate the bullet in his chest. Alexander knew that when electric telephone equipment came near metal it caused a buzzing sound. He tested his theory on former soldiers and found that his metal detector could identify which men still had bullets in their bodies. Unfortunately, the device failed on the president, who died. It would have worked were it not for the metal springs in Garfield's mattress, which Alexander was not aware of!

FLYING MACHINES

Alexander was fascinated by flying machines. In 1909, he helped develop an airplane named the *Silver Dart*, which flew for half a mile in Baddeck, Nova Scotia, at a record-breaking speed of 40 miles per hour (64 kph). He also developed a tetrahedron kite. A tetrahedron is made up of four equilateral triangles and it is one of the most stable structures in the world. Alexander's later kites were so strong they could even carry a person.

The Word Is...

Alexander was an inventor who was always working on new ideas. He explained his passion for inventing:

"The inventor looks upon the world and is not contented with things as they are. He wants to improve whatever he sees, he wants to benefit the world; he is haunted by an idea. The spirit of invention possesses him, seeking materialization."

LATER YEARS

Alexander was interested in technology and new inventions until the very end of his life, but he never stopped working to help people with hearing difficulties. In 1893, he sold his share in Volta Associates and used the money to build the Volta Laboratory and Bureau in Washington, a center of research and information for the deaf and hard of hearing.

OLD FRIENDS

Alexander invented many things, but remained proud of his telephone. In 1915, he flew to New York City to be part of the grand opening of the transcontinental telephone line connecting the east and west coasts of the United States. Speaking from New York City to his former assistant Thomas Watson in San Francisco, Alexander repeated the first words he spoke on a telephone: "Mr. Watson, come here, I want to see you!" Watson replied: "It would take me a week to get to you this time!"

ALEXANDER'S LAST GREAT INVENTION

Between 1910 and 1911, Alexander toured the world. While he was away, he rode on a hydrofoil boat. Back at his estate in Nova Scotia, he and his assistant designed and built a boat named *Hydrodome number 4* or *HD-4*. It used a set of four underwater "wings" to lift it clear of the water's surface to help it to go faster. In 1919, the *HD-4* set a new world marine speed record of 70.86 miles per hour (114.04 kph), a record that remained unbeaten for 20 years!

Alexander designed hydrofoils similar to this one. This hydrofoil is lifted high above the water.

Alexander and Decibels

The volume of different sounds is measured in units called decibels (dB). The term was created in the early days of the telephone as a way to measure cable and equipment performance. Decibel is actually two words: deci, meaning one-tenth, and bel, named after Alexander Graham Bell, which is why the "B" is always written in uppercase: "dB."

TELEPHONE TRIBUTES

Alexander died on August 2, 1922, at his home in Baddeck, Nova Scotia. He died from complications related to diabetes, a condition he suffered from. Shortly before he died, it is reported that Mabel said, "Don't leave me." Unable to speak, he replied, "No" in sign language. During his funeral, all of the telephone services across the United States and Canada shut down for a minute as a tribute to Alexander and his incredible, world-changing invention.

Alexander and his wife Mabel hold hands. She remained by his side until the end of his life.

CHANGING THE WORLD

The telephone was, without a doubt, one of the most important inventions of the nineteenth century. The telephone was also an invention that spread rapidly. At the time of Alexander's death in 1922, more than one-third of homes in the United States owned a telephone and over 13 million telephones were in use across the world.

CAUSING CHANGE

New developments and advances improved telephones. In the 1950s, transatlantic cables were laid at the bottom the Atlantic Ocean to connect phones in the United States and United Kingdom. In 1973, the cell phone was invented. At first, these phones were large and heavy. However, because they worked without wires, for the first time people could speak to each other outside buildings. Telephones helped people do business with customers and other companies all around the world. Because people were able to speak to each other so easily, information spread quickly from country to country. The world became a smaller place.

The name "Bell" is still famous for phones. These public telephones are in Toronto, Canada, where Bell is still Canada's largest phone company.

TELEPHONES TODAY

Today, the telephone is so much a part of our everyday lives that most of us carry one with us at all times. Long ago, it could take days or weeks to send a message over a long distance. Now, we can be in touch with almost anyone, almost anywhere in the world at any time, day or night. We do not use phones just to talk to people. Many cell phones contain **GPS** systems too, so they can be used to plan routes or tell people their location if they are lost. We use our cell phones to take photos, play games, watch movies, listen to music, and access the Internet. It is difficult to know what Alexander Graham Bell would have thought of today's phones, but he would probably be delighted by just how much his invention changed the world.

Alexander would probably not recognize today's phones and would be amazed by the things they can do!

The Word Is...

From the earliest days of his invention, Alexander understood the huge potential of the telephone to change the world. In 1878, he wrote:

"I believe in the future wires will unite the head offices of telephone companies in different cities, and a man in one part of the country may communicate by word of mouth with another in a distant place."

27

TIMELINE

1837 Samuel Morse invents the first successful telegraph and Morse Code to send messages using his invention.

1856 Antonio Meucci makes a telephone system from his workshop to his wife's bedroom.

1876 Alexander Graham Bell gets the first patent for a successful telephone.

1876 Alexander demonstrates the telephone to Emperor Pedro II of Brazil at the Centennial Exhibition in Philadelphia.

1878 The first US telephone exchange opens in New Haven, under license from Bell Telephone.

Alexander, shown here in 1899 after inventing not only the telephone, but also the metal detector and the iron lung.

1914 The first telephone lines stretch across the United States.

1915 The opening ceremony of the transcontinental telephone line and the first transcontinental phone call takes place.

1919 Rotary-dial telephones make it easier for customers to place calls without an operator.

1929 Herbert Hoover becomes the first US president to have a phone on his desk.

1937 The first emergency calls are made on a telephone.

1949 The first phone that has a ringer and a handset is invented, with a volume control for the ringer.

1956 The first telephone cable is laid beneath the Atlantic Ocean to connect telephones in the United Kingdom and United States.

1962 The first communications satellite, *Telstar 1*, is launched, transmitting the first live telephone and data signals.

1963 The push-button telephone is introduced.

1964 The first working video phones are invented, allowing users to see as well as speak with the person on the other end of a telephone.

1968 The first emergency 911 call is made in the United States.

1970 The first videophones are sold to the public.

1973 The first cellular phone is invented by American inventor Martin Cooper.

1978 Two thousand new cellular phones are given out to test how they work.

1980s Portable phones are available for people to buy and use in their homes.

1992 The world's first commercial text message is sent.

1995 The text messaging service, known as Short Message Service (SMS), is launched.

1999 The first cell phones that can send email and use the Internet are launched.

2000 Camera phones go on sale for the first time

2002 The US House of Representatives recognize the role of the Antonio Meucci in the invention of the telephone.

2007 The iPhone becomes the first cell phone to have a touchscreen.

2009 There are more than 4 billion cell phones in use worldwide.

2012 More than 6 billion people, over three-quarters of the world's population, have access to a cell phone.

2014 The number of active cell phone accounts exceeds the world's population.

This plaque is one of many that have been put up to celebrate Alexander and his invention of the telephone.

ONE
BORN
2ND 1875
N SOCIETY
HE
LPHONE
COMPANY
ABLET
16

RICHAR

GLOSSARY

acid A substance that can be extremely harmful.

currents The flow of electricity through wires.

ear trumpet A device that helps people with hearing problems hear by collecting sound waves and leading them into the ear.

electricity A form of energy that makes machines work.

electromagnet A piece of metal that becomes magnetic when electricity passes through it.

elocution The study and practice of speaking.

GPS Stands for Global Positioning System, a system in which signals from a satellite are sent to a device on Earth to tell someone their exact location in the world.

investor A person who gives money to a project with the expectation of making money when that project is successful.

lipreading Understanding what someone is saying by watching the movements of their lips without hearing the sounds they are making.

Morse Code A series of long or short spaces between clicks, or dots, and dashes on a page, that stand for letters of the alphabet.

patent A document issued to someone who invents something new so that other people do not copy it without permission.

receiver A device that changes radio waves and other signals into sounds or pictures.

respirator A machine that helps people breathe.

telegraph A system of sending messages as electrical signals along wires.

transmitter The part of a telephone into which a person speaks.

vibrations Movements up and down or back and forth. When you hit a drum, the drum skin vibrates.

Books

Bader, Bonnie. *Who Was Alexander Graham Bell?* New York, NY: Grosset & Dunlap, 2013.

Chambers, Catherine. *The First Telephone* (DK Adventures). New York, NY: DK Children, 2015.

Lassieur, Allison. *Phones* (Amicus Readers: 100 Years Ago). Mankato, MN: Amicus, 2011.

Matthews, Tom L. *Always Inventing: A Photobiography of Alexander Graham Bell* (Photobiographies). Des Moines, IA: National Geographic, 2015.

Venezia, Mike. *Alexander Graham Bell: Setting the Tone for Communication* (Getting to Know the World's Greatest Inventors & Scientists). New York, NY: Children's Press, 2009.

Websites

Due to the changing nature of Internet links, PowerKids Press has developed an online list of websites related to the subject of this book. This site is updated regularly. Please use this link to access the list: **www.powerkidslinks.com/itctw/bell**

INDEX